MW01618412

The 3 Pigs
&
Barry the Big Butt Wolf

Author
Big G
(Gasologist)

Illustrations
David Green

Copyright © 2021 (Big G)
Illustrated by David Green
All rights reserved worldwide.

No part of the book may be copied or changed in any format, sold, or used in a way other than what is outlined in this book, under any circumstances, without the prior written permission of the publisher.

Publisher: Inspiring Publishers,
P.O. Box 159, Calwell, ACT Australia 2905
Email: publishaspg@gmail.com
http://www.inspiringpublishers.com

A catalogue record for this book is available from the National Library of Australia

National Library of Australia The Prepublication Data Service

Author: Big G
Title: The 3 Pigs & Barry the Big Butt Wolf
Genre: Children's Literature
ISBN: 978-1-922618-88-7

The 3 Pigs
&
Barry the Big Butt Wolf

Barry was a chubby wolf with a cuddly 'A' shaped body, who lived in an underground den with his parents Hazel and Maximus, who spent every day searching for food to feed his enormous appetite.

To keep Barry fed, Max would have to hunt every day while Hazel would gather berries and leaves to have enough to eat.

At this stage you are thinking that Barry is a young pup, but no, it was coming up to his fifth birthday and in wolf years he was about to turn thirty-five, and his dad Max was tired of his son's lazy life.

Wolf
DEN.

Hazel loved her son, but was often blown out of the den by Barry unleashing his atomic farts, which were often brewing all day from the amount of food he ate.

Wolf DEN.
FART

It was time to get Barry to start bringing home food for the family.

There was only one problem, their son did not know how to hunt, and even when Hazel took him out gathering berries and leaves Barry would fall asleep under the closest shady tree.

How were they going to get Barry to help with finding food?

Max and Hazel often tried to catch the 3 little pigs, but they were always able to stay safe in their houses made of straw, sticks and bricks.

The next day, as Hazel was again being blown out of the den by a Barry extra charged methane missile, she had an amazing thought as to how her son could help catch those little pigs!

Hazel told Max her great plan to catch the pigs. They would feed Barry heaps of food and aim his mega load of gas at the home of the first little pig's House of Straw.

Wolf DEN
IDEA!

The next day Hazel saw the first little pig rolling in his favourite mud puddle, so Max and Hazel chased the little bacon bullet back to his straw house, where he locked himself inside.

As planned, Barry was close to the House of Straw eating a basket full of food.

Max at the top of his voice yelled, "Come out little piggy or Barry will munch, and crunch and he will blow your house down."

HOUSE of STRAW

Little pig yelled back, “We are not coming out, you are not able to blow my house down!”

HOUSE of STRAW

Barry stuffed a few more mouthfuls of food down his throat, and like clockwork his stomach rumbled like thunder, and he then unleashed a butt splitting tornado which destroyed the straw house.

HOUSE of STRAW

Max and Hazel were so excited they both dived at the little pink porkers, but clashed heads and the little pigs quickly sprinted to the second little pig's home, made of sticks.

HA! HA!
BONK!

Disappointed, but still on a mission to catch those little pigs, Hazel moved her strike weapon, Big Butt Barry, right outside of the House of Sticks and filled the basket once again.

Max yelled at the top of his voice, “Barry will munch and crunch and blow your house down.”

This time there was no reply from inside as the 3 little pigs prepared for what was to follow.

Barry calmly aimed his backside in the general direction of the stick house, and with stealth accuracy vaporised the home with one almighty nuclear butt bomb.

HOUSE OF STICKS
- NO WOLVES ALLOWED
KA-BOOM

This time, Max and Hazel were not going to collide, they had a fishing net and were determined to swoop in and catch them all. But as the dust settled Hazel had caught someone but it was not the 3 little pigs, it was Max, and the little porkers scurried off to the House of Bricks.

HOUSE of STICKS
NO WOLVES ALLOWED
BOOM

The brick home was not going to blow down like the straw and stick houses, the three pigs were smiling back at the wolf family, knowing that even a hurricane would not demolish it.

HOUSE OF BRICKS

Hazel decided to bring out the top shelf fart fodder, and peeled three large rockmelons for Barry to gorge on. As the last slice of melon was choked down, there was a sub-woofer sized rumbling sound coming from his stomach which shook Max and Hazel like an earthquake!

Barry started to twitch and shake, then he began uncontrollable aerial cartwheels powered by a continuous air stream of mutant methane.

FART

Max and Hazel watched on with fear, hoping their only son was not going to explode before their eyes.

Barry then shot into the air like a skyrocket.

EARTH

Miraculously, Barry landed on the chimney of the brick house.

A moment of relief for both parents was replaced with more fear, as they could see Barry's stomach again swelling to gigantic proportions.

HOUSE OF BRICKS

Hazel knew exactly what to do, she went and grabbed a large net and had Max hold the other side in front of the brick house door, so when triple BBB released the sphincter seal down the chimney, the door would splinter and be followed by the three bacon banquets.

With a groan that a bullfrog would have been proud of, Barry delivered the motherlode and blew the 3 little pigs out the front door and into the waiting net.

BLAST

Barry, with his mum and dad, took the 3 little pigs home. But instead of eating them, Barry befriended them and taught them how to produce mega methane. They now wake up every morning, eat a massive breakfast and walk down the hill to their new jobs, inflating hot air balloons.

THE END